ACKNOWLEDGMENTS

Special thanks to David Branon of *Sports Spectrum* magazine, a publication dedicated to the Christian athlete, who was extremely helpful in providing leads for this book. Also I'm thankful to Linda Brown of Athletes in Action in Colorado Springs, Colorado for her suggestions and material. I can't thank Karl Schaller enough for providing this opportunity in the first place. And I'm especially thankful to my husband, Jerry Newcombe, for his invaluable help and encouragement with the entire project.

DEDICATION

To my son, Eric, who loves the Lord and is already a great athlete.

Library of Congress Cataloging-in-Publication Data

Newcombe, Kristi.
Athletes of faith/by Kristi Newcombe.
p. cm.
SUMMARY: Briefly introduces men and women who have won medals in the Olympics and who have also demonstrated their Christian faith through the way they live.
ISBN 0-7814-3021-6
1. Athletes–Religious live–Juvenile literature. 3. Olympics–Juvenile literature. (1. Athletes.
2. Olympics.) I. Title.
BV4596.A8 N48 1999
248.8'8–dc21

97-42696
CIP
AC

Chariot Victor Publishing
A division of Cook Communications, Colorado Springs, CO 80918
Cook Communications, Paris, Ontario
Kingsway Communications, Eastbourne, England

Athletes of Faith
© 1999 by Kirsti Sæbø Newcombe

First printing, 1999
Printed in United States of America
03 02 01 00 99   5 4 3 2 1

PHOTO CREDITS

Eric Liddell: Cover & Right, © Allsport; **David Robinson**: Cover, © Tony Warshaw/Allsport USA & Right, © Time, Inc.; **Paul Anderson**: Left & Right, courtesy of Paul Anderson Youth Home; **Dennis Byrd**: Right, © Mike Powell/Allsport USA; **Madeline Mims**: Left, © UPI/Corbis-Bettman; Right, © Tony Duffy/Allsport USA; **Janet Lynn**: Left & Right, © The World Figure Skating Museum; **Andre Dawson**: Right, © UPI/Corbis-Bettman; **David Johnson**: Left, © Mike Powell/Allsport USA; Right, © Simon Bruty/Allsport USA; **A.C. Green**: Right, © Stephen Dunn/Allsport USA; **Mary Ellen Clark**: Left, © Stu Forster/Allsport USA; Back Cover & Right, © Tony Duffy/Allsport USA; **Ruthie Bolton**: Cover & Right, © Al Bello/Allsport USA; **Beckey Dyroen-Lancer & Suzannah Bianco**: Left & Right, © Anne Hamersky

Athletes of FAITH

Kirsti Sæbø Newcombe

Chariot Victor Publishing
A Division of Cook Communications

Eric Liddell

Sport: Track and Field

Olympic Contest: 1924 Paris, France

400-meter—Gold Medal

200-meter—Bronze Medal

God made Eric so that he could run very fast. He could run faster than any boy or girl in Scotland, his home country. He won two medals in the Olympics.

Eric's father was a missionary to China. Eric also became a missionary to China later in his life. But first he spent time telling other athletes in the Olympics about the love of Jesus Christ. Eric believed that Christians need to be strong both in their bodies and in their hearts. He told everyone that he would not run on Sunday, because it is the Lord's day, and he would go to church instead.

David Robinson

Sport: NBA Basketball
Team: U.S. Naval Academy (1983-1987)
San Antonio Spurs (1989-present)
Olympic Contest: 1988 Seoul, Korea—Bronze Medal
1992 Barcelona, Spain—Gold Medal

Nobody thought David Robinson would grow up to be an NBA superstar. He was too busy reading, solving math problems, or assembling big-screen TVs. But while he was in the Naval Academy, David grew to 7'1", and people began calling him "The Admiral" because of his spectacular command of the basketball court. From there, his incredible athletic ability took him on to a career as center for the San Antonio Spurs, where he won awards for Rookie of the Year and Most Valuable Player. He played with the United States Olympic basketball team twice and won an Olympic bronze and gold medal.

It dawned on him, "I can have all the material things in the world, but they mean nothing if my soul, my spiritual side, is empty." He was scared. He thought, "Without the Lord, I have nothing. All the money, everything I have—without him, I have nothing." He closed his eyes and prayed. "Everything you've given me," he told the Lord, "I'm giving back to you today."

Paul Anderson

Sport: Weight Lifting

Olympic Contest: 1956 Melbourne, Australia—Gold Medal

Weightlifters must be very strong, and Paul was a strong Christian as well as a strong man. When he went to the Olympics in 1956, he weighed 303 pounds (or 138 kg). Paul had a bad throat infection, called strep, on the day of his competition. Even though he felt very sick, he still won the gold medal by lifting 1099 1/2 pounds (or 500 kg). Can you imagine lifting something that weighs three times more than you?

Paul Anderson loved kids. He shared Jesus' love with them by opening his home to many kids who were in trouble or who had no family or home of their own.

Today, the Paul Anderson Youth Home is still a safe place for teenage boys in Vidalia, Georgia.

"Your Friend in Christ"

IF WE LOVE ONE ANOTHER,
GOD ABIDES IN US.....AND
HIS LOVE IS PERFECTED
US.

I JOHN 4:12

Dennis Byrd

Sport: NFL Football
Team: New York Jets (1989-1992)

A moment in time—a split-second collision with a 280-pound teammate—and Dennis Byrd lay paralyzed, his neck shattered. Suddenly, what mattered in life was no longer football. It was whether he'd ever walk again. Dennis overcame his paralyzing injury and, with the help of his wife and dedicated physical therapists, learned to walk again. There is a verse in 2 Corinthians about weakness that spoke to Dennis: "My grace is sufficient for you, for my power is made perfect in weakness."

Dennis thought, "Only in my weakness was I able to lay my entire life at Christ's feet. He had to fight the battle for me, and He did. I feared I would never have my legs beneath me again; they are here now, and they will only get stronger. There could be no better answer to what Satan tried to do to me than to walk out onto that football stadium turf for the Jets' opening-day game. I have taken that walk. I always knew I would."

Dennis Byrd lives with his wife and children in Owaso, Oklahoma. Dennis' primary activity is operating the Dennis Byrd Foundation which was created to build and operate a summer camp for children with disabilities. For more information, write the Dennis Byrd Foundation, PO Box 90, Owaso, Oklahoma, 74055. Phone number, (918) 274-1332 or fax (918) 274-1323.

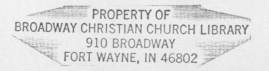

Madeline Mims

Sport: Track and Field

Olympic Contest: 1968 Mexico City, Mexico
800-meter—Gold Medal
1972 Munich, Germany
400-meter relay—Silver Medal

Madeline grew up in a ghetto in Cleveland, Ohio. Her family had no father in the home, they were poor, and life was very hard. When she was twelve years old, she heard that another black girl, Wilma Rudolph, had won a gold medal at the Olympics. Madeline knew that she was a fast runner too. She could run faster than any of the other kids around.

A dream was born in Madeline's heart. She trained very hard and became a member of the U.S. Olympic Team four times. In 1968 she set a world record and won the gold medal in the 800-meter race.

Madeline always talks about God, and she has given her life in service to Him. She speaks and sings to audiences all over, and she writes to tell people about Jesus. In the 1996 Olympics in Atlanta, Georgia, she ministered to the athletes and to her fellow chaplains.

Janet Lynn

Sport: Figure Skating

Olympic Contest: 1972 Sapporo, Japan—Bronze Medal

Janet wore ice skates for the first time when she was two years old. She fell over and over, but she loved gliding on the ice. She asked her mother constantly to take her skating.

As she grew, Janet won many championships. She often fell, but she always got up and kept skating. During her performances, she would smile her radiant, beautiful smile and wave to the crowds. Her strong faith in Christ always kept her going.

At the 1972 Olympics, Janet did well during the first part of her performance, even through all of the difficult parts. Suddenly she fell during a relatively easy "sit spin." She could have stopped right there, but she got up, finished her performance, and placed third, winning the bronze medal.

Andre Dawson

Sport: Baseball
Teams: Montreal Expos (1976-1986), Chicago Cubs (1987-1992), Boston Red Sox (1993-1994), Florida Marlins (1995-1996)
Achievements: 1977 National League Rookie of the Year. 1980 & 1984 Golden Glove winner.

Andre Dawson grew up without a father in a poor family. But his grandmother taught him something that would change his life: She taught him about God. With the love and support of his family, Andre began to pursue his dream. From a junior league to high-school baseball to the minor leagues, Andre never doubted God's plan for his life. And finally, in 1977, his dream came true, he signed on with the Montreal Expos.

Andre says today, "Go when the Lord calls, wherever and whenever He calls. Go whether you understand why He is calling or not. Just go. For each one of us is important to Him, and each one of us has a purpose that only He knows."

David Johnson

Sport: Track and Field

Olympic Contest: 1992 Barcelona, Spain

Decathlon—Bronze Medal

As a boy growing up, Dave always seemed to get into trouble. One day, when he was in high school, Dave finally prayed this prayer: "Lord, please don't give up on me." God heard his prayer and helped give Dave direction for his life. He worked hard, and, with God's help, Dave became one of the best athletes in the world.

The Decathlon is a very hard series of ten athletic events, including running and different kinds of jumping and throwing. It is one of the hardest of all Olympic events. David has completed not one, but many, decathlons. Right before the 1992 Olympics, Dave broke his foot! Even though it was painful, he still wanted to compete, so he entered the Decathlon. He kept on running, jumping, and throwing, and finished the contest on his broken foot.

Dave got the bronze medal, but he knew he had a "gold medal" in God's eyes. When things were difficult, Dave Johnson did not give up. He did his best for God.

A.C. Green

Sport: NBA Basketball
Teams: Los Angeles Lakers (1985-1993), Phoenix Suns
      (1993-1996), Dallas Mavericks (1996-present)
Achievements: 1984 Pac-10 Player of the year.
      Voted to 1990 All Star Game.

A.C. Green has played with basketball's greatest stars: Kareem Abdul-Jabbar, Magic Johnson, Charles Barkley, and others. He has competed in the NBA finals four times and won two championships with the Lakers. And he now plays for the Dallas Mavericks.

Instead of bowing to peer pressure, A.C. Green stands for sexual purity and integrity. Instead of spending his money on cars and fancy clothes, A.C. Green uses his money to disciple young athletes and help kids reach their potential.

A.C. says, "Years ago, before I accepted Christ, I thought I was a good guy. I sat in church, did good things, and made fresh resolutions every New Year's Day. But before I met Christ, I was not in the kingdom of light but in the kingdom of darkness. I needed help. I needed Jesus."

Mary Ellen Clark

Sport: Platform Diving

Olympic Contest: 1992 Barcelona, Spain—Bronze Medal
1996 Atlanta, Georgia, U.S.A.—Bronze Medal

Mary Ellen learned how to trust in God when she was just a little girl. She also learned how to dive at a young age. She loved to dive, and practiced until she became a very good diver. But over the years Mary Ellen began to get dizzy when she dove. Her dizziness got worse and worse, and for a while she thought she would have to give up diving. But God helped her get over her dizziness, and she earned two Olympic medals for diving.

When Mary Ellen dives off a 33-foot platform, she remembers what faith and trust in God are all about.

Ruthie Bolton

Sport: WNBA Basketball
Team: Sacramento Monarchs
Olympic Contest: 1996 Atlanta, Georgia, U.S.A.—Gold Medal

Ruthie grew up in a large family, with nineteen brothers and sisters. Her father was a pastor. She loves to play basketball, but the most important thing in her life is to please God. Ruthie tried out for the 1992 Olympic team but did not make it. But she didn't give up. She tried again, and in 1996 she did make the team, and they won the gold medal. Now, she plays professional women's basketball.

Basketball is not Ruthie's only talent. She also sings gospel songs and has recorded a CD with her nineteen brothers and sisters and all sixty-seven of her nieces and nephews!

Beckey Dyroen-Lancer and Suzannah Bianco

Event: Synchronized Swimming
Olympic Contest: 1996 Atlanta, Georgia, U.S.A.—Gold Medal

These two swimming sisters believe that victory means going alongside one another and doing your best for the glory of God.

According to the experts, Beckey is the best synchronized swimmer in the world. Synchronized swimming is like doing a ballet dance in the water, without touching the bottom of the pool. These athletes have to be excellent in swimming, gymnastics, and ballet. Beckey's husband, Kevin, is a former ballet dancer, and he helps her when she practices her routines. Kevin and Beckey met in church, and they love God very much.

Suzannah is also an excellent synchronized swimmer. She is married to a pastor, and she always encourages everyone to be kind and serve one another.

Beckey and Suzannah were both on the synchronized swimming team that won the gold medal in Atlanta.

Athletes of Faith

AGE: 5-10

LIFE ISSUE: My child chooses heroes and role models that don't exhibit Christian values.

VALUE: Choosing good role models.

Parent Interactivity: Read a story from this book with your child, then choose an activity to help reinforce the value of choosing good role models. Try to choose activities that use your child's primary learning style.

Visual Learning Style: (I learn with my eyes.) Help your child create an album for his or her sport heroes and other role models. Use the project to discuss the importance of choosing role models who practice Christian values and try to honor God with their lives. Use a picture album and include such things as newspaper and magazine clippings and pictures. If you keep your eyes open you can find positive, value-enforcing stories about athletes and other heroes on a regular basis. Encourage your child to adopt as role models some or all of the athletes featured in this book. Feel free to copy parts of their stories into your child's "Hero Album."

Auditory Learning Style: (I learn with my ears.) After each story, spend a significant amount of time discussing how and why you admire the featured athlete for taking a stand for his or her faith. Let your child tell you why he or she admires the athlete. Occasionally take the opportunity to write a story about your child—you can write these stories about things that actually happened to your child, or frame them as if they are taking place in the future to cast vision for what your child can do and become. Always stress the character your child exhibits. For example, after your child scores a winning touchdown in a football game, write a story that celebrates both his achievement and his character that made him a hero, including made-up quotes from some of his role models.

Tactile Learning Style: (I learn by doing things.) If your child is a tactile learner, be creative and dream up hands-on projects or object lessons that reinforce the importance of choosing role models with strong Christian character. Here is an idea: Take a small box and cover it completely with frosting so no part of the box can be seen. Tell your child you have a special treat for him or her, then look surprised when he or she tries to eat it and becomes disappointed that there is no cake! Take out a real piece of cake. Discuss the idea that what any person does is just the "frosting" of life; who that person is, or how strong their character is, is the "cake," or substance, of life.

Sources

BOOKS

Akers, Michelle and Nelson, Judith A., *Face to Face with Michelle Akers* (Orlando, FL: Success Factors, 1996).

Eikje, Ove, *Mer enn Gull (More than Gold)*, (Oslo, Norway: Lunde Forlag, 1992).

Johnson, Dave, *Aim High* (Grand Rapids, MI: Zondervan Publishing House, 1994).

Nelson, Rebecca and MacNee, Marie J. *The Olympic Factbook* (Detroit: Visible Ink Press, 1996).

Reed and Salaza, editors, *Great Athletes of the Twentieth Century* (Pasadena, CA: Magill Books, Salem Press, 1992), vols. 10, 11, 15.

Wallechinsky, David, *Sports Illustrated Presents: The Complete Book of the Summer Olympics* (Boston: Little, Brown & Co., 1996).

The World Almanac 1997 (Mahwah, NJ: World Almanac Books, 1996).

Chariot Victor Publishing would like to thank Zondervan Publishing for granting permission to use the following books: *Today's Heroes: A.C. Green, Today's Heroes: David Robinson, Today's Heroes: Andrew Dawson.*

MAGAZINES

Sports Spectrum, June 1996. (Grand Rapids, MI: Discovery House Publishers). Article on: David Robinson p. 14, Ruthie Bolton p. 6, Madeline Mims p. 30.

Campus Life, May/June 1996. Article on Dave Johnson p. 34.

Guideposts, Jan. 1997. Cover story on Mary Ellen Clark p. 4

Virtue, July/August 1996. Cover story on Suzannah Bianco and Becky Dyroen-Lancer p. 26.